In
1935 if you wanted to
read a good book, you needed
either a lot of money or a library card.
Cheap paperbacks were available, but their
poor production generally mirrored the quality
between the covers. One weekend that year,
Allen Lane, Managing Director of The Bodley Head,
having spent the weekend visiting Agatha Christie,
found himself on a platform at Exeter station trying to
find something to read for his journey back to London.
He was appalled by the quality of the material he had to
choose from. Everything that Allen Lane achieved from that
day until his death in 1970 was based on a passionate belief
in the existence of 'a vast reading public for *intelligent*
books at a low price'. The result of his momentous vision
was the birth not only of Penguin, but of the 'paperback
revolution'. Quality writing became available for the price of
a packet of cigarettes, literature became a mass medium
for the first time, a nation of book-borrowers became a
nation of book-buyers – and the very concept of book
publishing was changed for ever. Those founding
principles – of quality and value, with an overarching
belief in the fundamental importance of reading –
have guided everything the company has
done since 1935. Sir Allen Lane's
pioneering spirit is still very much alive
at Penguin in 2005. Here's to
the next 70 years!

The Aristocratic
Adventurer

DAVID CANNADINE

PENGUIN BOOKS

PENGUIN BOOKS

Published by the Penguin Group
Penguin Books Ltd, 80 Strand, London WC2R ORL, England
Penguin Group (USA) Inc., 375 Hudson Street, New York, New York 10014, USA
Penguin Group (Canada), 10 Alcorn Avenue, Toronto, Ontario, Canada M4V 3B2
(a division of Pearson Penguin Canada Inc.)
Penguin Ireland, 25 St Stephen's Green, Dublin 2, Ireland
(a division of Penguin Books Ltd)
Penguin Group (Australia), 250 Camberwell Road, Camberwell, Victoria 3124,
Australia (a division of Pearson Australia Group Pty Ltd)
Penguin Books India Pvt Ltd, 11 Community Centre,
Panchsheel Park, New Delhi – 110 017, India
Penguin Group (NZ), cnr Airborne and Rosedale Roads, Albany,
Auckland 1310, New Zealand (a division of Pearson New Zealand Ltd)
Penguin Books (South Africa) (Pty) Ltd, 24 Sturdee Avenue,
Rosebank 2196, South Africa

Penguin Books Ltd, Registered Offices: 80 Strand, London WC2R ORL, England

www.penguin.com

Aspects of Aristocracy first published by Yale University Press 1994
Published in Penguin Books 1995
This extract published as a Pocket Penguin 2005

1

Set in 11/13pt Monotype Dante
Typeset by Palimpsest Book Production Limited
Polmont, Stirlingshire
Printed in England by Clays Ltd, St Ives plc

was regarded – and regretted – by observers as emphatic sign of his upper-class origins. He considered servants and secretaries, gardeners and gamekeepers, horses and hounds, to be integral parts of the natural order of things. He had no understanding of the minds or mores of the middle classes, and it cannot be coincidence that so many of his political adversaries came from that social background: Joseph and Neville Chamberlain, Bonar Law, Stanley Baldwin and Clement Attlee. He knew virtually nothing of the lives of the ordinary men and women who made up the majority of Britain's population. He never went into a shop, or travelled on a bus, and on the one occasion when he journeyed on the underground, he got on the Circle Line and went helplessly round and round on it until, several hours later, a friend rescued him from the ordeal. Even as late as 1951, he still believed that most people in Britain lived in 'cottage homes': a phrase which revealingly mingles his paternal benevolence with his aristocratic ignorance.

In retrospect, Churchill liked to present himself as a deprived and disadvantaged child, further handicapped by a minimal education, who achieved renown in the world by his own unaided efforts. But while there can be no doubting his ambition and his application, it is also clear that in the early stages of his career, he shamelessly exploited his aristocratic connections with single-minded purpose and success. As a soldier hungry for action and glory, he secured postings to the Indian frontier and the Sudan, thanks not merely to his own tireless lobbying, but also to that of his mother, who, he later recalled, furthered his plans and guarded his interests 'with all her influence and boundless energy'. By the same means, he obtained the best prices for his reporting of the Boer War, and the most generous advances for his early books. When he began his political career as a Conservative candidate, his cousin the Duke of Marlborough helped to pay his election expenses. When he crossed the floor of the Commons, he was invited to contest Manchester North-West thanks to the intervention of his uncle, Lord Tweedmouth, who happened to be a senior figure in the Liberal Party. In some senses, young Winston may have been a self-made man; but he was also, by birth and connection, a member of Britain's charmed inner circle, and he early on learned how to pull its strings to his own advantage.

Yet there was another side to Churchill's patrician persona which deserves much fuller exploration than it has so far received. At the outset of his career, he certainly benefited from the patronage and support of his noble connections. But in the much longer perspective of his ninety-year lifetime, the aristocracy was a declining force in British politics, in British society, and in British history, and Churchill himself was very much an aristocrat of his time. Like many late nineteenth-century patricians, his immediate family background was impoverished, unstable, and tainted by scandal, and some of his distant relatives were even more accident-prone or disreputable. As with many well-born men of his generation, his own finances were exceptionally precarious, and he was often in debt and beholden to those much richer than himself. Like other impoverished aristocrats, he was driven to writing for the newspapers, and to producing pious works of family history. And in his inconsistent opinions, his uncertain party loyalty, his disillusion with democracy, and his admiration for authoritarian forms of government, Churchill was behaving like many disoriented notables who had lost their bearings in the unfriendly and unfamiliar world of twentieth-century mass politics.

When placed against this broader historical background of widespread aristocratic decline, Churchill emerges as a much more palpable product of his class and his time than is often realised. And as far as his political career before 1940 was concerned, this was on balance a hindrance to him rather than a help. His blue blood may have been of use at the outset, but thereafter it increasingly became a liability. For it was not just that Churchill was widely distrusted as a man of unstable temperament, unsound judgement, and rhetorical (and also alcoholic) excess. Nor even that his record in public life – Tonypandy, Antwerp, the Dardanelles, Chanak, Russia, the General Strike, India – was uniquely controversial. It was also that for most of his career, there hung around him an unsavoury air of disreputability and unseemliness, as a particularly wayward, rootless and anachronistic product of a decaying and increasingly discredited aristocratic order. Before 1940, it was not easy for him to be taken seriously as the man of destiny he believed himself to be, when so many people in the know regarded him as little better than an ungentlemanly, almost déclassé, adventurer.

Although he took the greatest pride in the ducal blood that pulsed through his veins, Churchill's family and forebears were hardly those which any politician eager to establish an unimpeachable public reputation would freely have chosen. For there were skeletons a-plenty rattling in the Marlborough family cupboard. The first duke may have been a 'heaven-born general', but he was also a man of dubious political and personal morality. Indeed, many Victorians, brought up on Macaulay, regarded him as disreputable and untrustworthy: he had betrayed James II and conspired against William III, and he had pursued power and wealth with unscrupulous and single-minded ardour. Since then, the Marlboroughs had been either unhappy or undistinguished or both. Many of them had been unstable, depressive and bad-tempered. The third, fourth and fifth dukes were profligate even by the standards of the late eighteenth and early nineteenth centuries, and none of them had played a significant part in the affairs of their time. Indeed, Gladstone's harsh words of 1882 probably expressed the generally held late-Victorian view: 'There never was a Churchill from John of Marlborough down that had either morals or principles.' And for the next fifty-eight years, that remained the conventional wisdom on the subject.

By the last quarter of the nineteenth century, therefore, the Marlboroughs seemed to be heading rapidly and almost self-destructively downhill. In marked contrast to his predecessors, Churchill's grandfather, the seventh duke, who inherited the title in 1857, was a pious and high-minded Victorian nobleman, and his wife was the formidable Lady Frances Anne, daughter of the third Lord Londonderry. But by mid-nineteenth-century ducal standards the Marlboroughs were far from rich, and the accumulated extravagances of his predecessors meant that the seventh duke inherited the estates in parlous condition. As a result, he was reluctantly compelled to disperse much of the patrimony he would have wished to safeguard. In 1862, he sold the family estates in Wiltshire and Shropshire, and twelve years later he parted with his Buckinghamshire holdings to Baron Ferdinand de Rothschild for £220,000. Heirlooms went the same way as ancestral acres: in 1875, the Marlborough gems were auctioned for thirty-five thousand guineas, and in the early 1880s, the magnificent Sunderland Library was disposed of for £56,581, after the necessary special legislation had been obtained from Parliament.

This process of dispersal was continued by the eighth duke, Churchill's uncle, who succeeded in 1883, and soon parted with most of the magnificent collection of Blenheim Old Masters, for £350,000. There the resemblance between father and son ended, for the eighth duke was one of the most disreputable men ever to have debased the highest rank in the British peerage. As a youth he was expelled from Eton, and soon acquired a well-deserved reputation for being rude, erratic, profligate, irresponsible and lacking in self-control. In 1876, his affair with the already married Lady Aylesford became a public scandal; the Prince of Wales branded him 'the greatest blackguard alive'; and in 1881 he fathered by her an illegitimate child. Two years later, his first wife divorced him, and the new duke's social disgrace was complete. In 1886, he figured prominently in the sensational divorce case featuring Lady Colin Campbell, his one-time mistress, and shortly after he married a rich American, Lilian Hammersley, which enabled him to install electric light and central heating at Blenheim. Appropriately enough, the eighth duke's politics were as wayward as his libido. During the early 1880s, he was successively a Liberal, an Extreme Radical and a Conservative, and he produced a series of equally confused articles, calling for the reform of the Lords and of the land laws, and the preservation of 'a class of hereditarily trained statesmen connected with the land'. He died, as he had lived, in the tradition of a Gothic villain, being discovered in his laboratory at Blenheim 'with a terrible expression on his face'.

This was the unhappy state of affairs that 'Sunny' Marlborough, Churchill's cousin, sought to remedy during his long tenure as ninth duke, from 1892 to 1934; but he met with only very limited success. In politics, his career fizzled out: he held minor office under Salisbury and Balfour from 1899 to 1905, voted against the Parliament Bill in 1911, and by the inter-war years had become a paranoid and anti-semitic reactionary. In matrimony, he fared no better. His first marriage, to Consuelo Vanderbilt, was blatantly arranged for the money; they separated in 1906 and divorced in 1920. His second wife, Gladys Deacon, was a Bohemian adventuress, who had previously been his mistress. But marriage soured their relationship, and they separated in 1931. In financial terms, the Vanderbilt millions enabled the duke to restore the gardens and terraces at Blenheim, but by the end of his life he was on the brink of selling the family archives to Yale University, and he died virtually insolvent. And in social terms, the Marlboroughs remained unacceptable. The breakdown of the duke's two marriages was widely publicised, as was his admission into the Roman Catholic Church. Neither King

Edward VII nor King George V would receive him at court, nor would they accept from him the annual gift of the Blenheim flag. Most duchesses refused to recognise his second wife, and in Oxford county and episcopal society the duke himself was regarded with scarcely concealed disdain.

In the course of his short and tragic life, Churchill's father, Lord Randolph, was even more notorious. From his days as an Oxford undergraduate, he had shown an unhealthy delight in gambling, in drinking, and in overspending. His marriage to another American, Jennie Jerome, was accompanied by unseemly wrangles over money; by the early 1880s, he was heavily in debt and in thrall to money-lenders and company promoters; and at the end of his life, he owed the Rothschilds nearly £70,000. Like so many Churchills, only more so, his temperament was erratic and uncontrollable, and it seems almost certain that he contracted syphilis, which led to the general paralysis which slowly and humiliatingly killed him. In society, the Churchills were publicly ostracised between 1876 and 1884, after Lord Randolph had impulsively taken his elder brother's part in the row with the Prince of Wales over the Aylesford scandal. In politics, he was widely regarded as an unstable and unprincipled adventurer, whose vituperative style earned the condemnation of both Gladstone and Salisbury. His abrupt resignation as Chancellor of the Exchequer in January 1887 merely confirmed the widely held view that he was an unscrupulous menace, so unbalanced as to be almost insane. When, at the end of his maiden speech in the Commons, young Winston described his father as 'a certain splendid memory', many MPs must have found it difficult to recognise the very different Lord Randolph they themselves had known.

Churchill's mother was no less unrespectable. Although renowned for her beauty, and much admired for her public loyalty to Lord Randolph during his last pitiful years, she was as spendthrift, wayward and irresponsible as her husband. Their marriage soon became one of convenience only, it was widely known that she was having many affairs (especially with Count Charles Kinsky), and in 1886–7 there were frequent rumours that they were on the brink of divorce. After Lord Randolph's death she showed no inclination to moderate her ways, and in 1898 was obliged to raise a loan of £17,000 to clear her debts. Her response to this financial crisis was a commonplace one for aristocratic ladies in her condition. She briefly edited a magazine, the *Anglo-Saxon Review* (it made no money), and she wrote her reminiscences: but on her own admission, they were 'interesting chiefly in what is left unsaid'. In 1900, after a long affair, she married George Cornwallis-West. But he was twenty years younger than she was, scarcely older than Winston himself. In society, the union was widely condemned; it soon broke down; and it ended in divorce thirteen years later. Undaunted, she married her third husband, Montagu Porch, who was also twenty years her junior. Once again, her behaviour was generally regarded with derision, incredulity and astonishment.

By contrast, Churchill's wife, Clementine Hozier, whom he married in 1908, was high-minded, and endowed with much sounder judgement of men and events than her husband. Far from being the wealthy heiress whose fortune might have helped Churchill's political career, however, Clementine had spent her early life in genteel poverty. Her father, Henry Hozier – who was probably not her father at all – was an unsavoury and unattractive character, who had divorced her mother, Blanche, and left the family pitifully short of money. As the daughter of the Earl of Airlie, Blanche was herself descended from one of the more impoverished of Scotland's great families. Indeed, the household was so poor that Clementine could scarcely afford to take part in the expensive pageant of London high society, and before she met and married Winston she earned money by giving French lessons at 2s 6d an hour. To make matters worse, Blanche Hozier was not only an adultress, but also an incorrigible gambler, and this latter trait was inherited by Clementine's sister, Nellie, and her brother, William. In 1921, after having resolved to give up gambling altogether, Bill Hozier commited suicide in a cheap Paris hotel. Nor was this the first such scandal that Clementine had to live down: before she was betrothed to Winston, she had already been twice engaged, and in 1909, when Lord Percy, heir to the Duke of Northumberland, was found dead in Paris, it was whispered that he had been a former lover of Clementine's, and that he had been murdered on Churchill's instructions.

The person who was rumoured – quite without foundation – to have carried out this astonishing deed was Churchill's younger brother Jack (who was in fact inoffensive and self-effacing, and took no part in public affairs). Winston remained close to him all his life but, as this story suggests, Jack became the subject of gossip that did his elder brother's reputation no good. In appearance, and in temperament, they were markedly unalike, and it was widely (but mistakenly) believed that Jack and Winston were only half-brothers, and that the fifth Earl of Roden was in fact Jack's father. After all, it was generally known that Lady Randolph had had many affairs in the course of her first marriage, and her husband abstained from sexual relations with her once syphilis had been diagnosed. In an attempt to make some much-needed money, Jack took up a career as a stockbroker. But in the early twentieth century, this was still thought by many to be an unsuitable career for a gentleman, and in 1907 Jack had to postpone his marriage to Lady Gwendeline Bertie, because her mother, the Countess of Abingdon, thought his financial resources inadequate. Nor was this the last time that Jack's profession got him into trouble. When Churchill became Chancellor of the Exchequer, it was mildly awkward that his brother dealt in stocks and shares, and during the Second World War he was criticised for housing Jack in 10 Downing Street after his own London home had been bombed, and for keeping him as a permanent member of his Prime Ministerial entourage.

But this was as nothing compared with the embarrassment that Churchill had been caused, during the 1930s, by his three children, Randolph, Diana and Sarah. They were ill-disciplined, rowed with their parents, and all became heavy drinkers. In 1932, Diana married John Bailey, son of Sir Abe Bailey, a South African mining magnate and friend of her father's. Both her parents were opposed to the marriage, and it ended in divorce three years later. In 1935, Diana married Duncan Sandys, but they, too, were later divorced, and in 1963, she committed suicide. Her younger sister Sarah sought a career in the theatre, and in 1935 became a chorus girl in one of C. B. Cochrane's reviews. While on the stage, she fell in love with Vic Oliver, a twice-divorced, Austrian-born comedian, who was seventeen years older than she was. Her parents were determined to prevent her marriage to this 'itinerant vagabond', but Sarah ran off to join Oliver in New York, and they were duly married on Christmas Day 1936. On both sides of the Atlantic, the publicity was extensive and adverse, and did Churchill no good in political circles. In the autumn of 1938, when the Camrose press was campaigning for his return to the Cabinet, *Truth* wickedly suggested that if Vic Oliver was also made a minister, the comedy turn would then be complete. It was a jibe that Churchill neither forgave nor forgot.

But even Diana and Sarah seemed almost angelic compared to their rude, spoiled, unstable, headstrong, irresponsible and argumentative brother, Randolph. He dropped out of Oxford University, took to drinking and gambling, got into debt, and became notorious as the most dangerous and boorish party guest in London. For a time, he was much attracted by the ideas of Oswald Mosley and the New Party, and later wrote a newspaper column in which he championed his father's views on India with a tactless fervour that can only have been counter-productive. But it was Randolph's active political interventions which did Winston the greatest damage in the eyes of the Tory leadership and the National Government. Early in 1935, he stood at the Wavertree by-election as an unofficial Conservative candidate, on a Diehard platform. It was a sensational campaign, in which Randolph was attacked as a dissipated Mosleyite, and the result was to split the Tory vote and hand over a safe seat to Labour. A month later, he supported a second unofficial and ill-chosen Conservative candidate at Toxteth East: Richard Findlay, a former member of the British Union of Fascists. In January 1936, Randolph himself stood – again unsuccessfully – in a much-publicised by-election at Ross and Cromarty, against Malcolm MacDonald, who was not only a member of the National Government, but also the son of the former Prime Minister Ramsay MacDonald.

Despite their dynastic delinquencies, Churchill's fierce loyalty to his immediate family was one of his most endearing qualities. Like most patricians he sought, when able, to further his relatives' interests with the same zeal that they had earlier shown in promoting his own. Indeed, both Lady Violet Bonham Carter and Sir John Colville believed that Churchill's besetting sin was the appropriately aristocratic one of nepotism. When only a junior Conservative MP, he unsuccessfully tried to persuade the Colonial Secretary, Joseph Chamberlain, to appoint the ninth Duke of Marlborough Governor-General of Australia; and in 1915 he waged a persistent campaign to ensure that, despite his separation from Consuelo, the Duke should be appointed Lord Lieutenant of Oxfordshire. Although he deeply disapproved of Randolph 'leading the life of a selfish exploiter, borrowing and spending every shilling you can lay your hands upon', he did his utmost to help him. One friend, Professor Lindemann, procured a place at Christ Church, Oxford, while two more, Lord Beaverbrook and Brendan Bracken, found him jobs in journalism. In 1933, Churchill paid off £1,600 of his son's debts, and later went to speak on his behalf at Wavertree (though not at Ross and Cromarty).

But it cannot have helped Churchill's reputation that so many members of his immediate family were so often in the newspapers for such unedifying reasons. In every generation, among his closest relatives, there were too many debts, too much gambling, too much drinking. Even by the relatively lax standards of the Edwardian era or the inter-war years, there was an above-average amount of infidelity, divorce, erratic behaviour, sexual scandal, social ostracism and court disfavour. Thus described, the Marlboroughs were a textbook case of a declining and degenerate ducal dynasty: Lord Randolph might have stepped straight from the pages of Trollope's *The Way We Live Now*, the ninth duke was a character of almost Proustian pitifulness, and the headline-stealing antics of Diana, Sarah and Randolph might have been taken from a novel by Evelyn Waugh – with whom, appropriately enough, Randolph enjoyed a lifelong love-hate relationship. This only reinforced the prevailing view that *all* the Churchills were unstable, unsound and untrustworthy: utterly devoid, as Gladstone had damningly observed, of either morals or principles.

Surrounded as he was by such unsavoury relatives, it is easy to see why many contemporaries concluded that Churchill himself was equally disreputable and unreliable. In 1885, the fifteenth Earl of Derby had dismissed Lord Randolph as 'thoroughly untrustworthy: scarcely a gentleman and probably more or less mad'. Thirty years later, Derby's nephew described Lord Randolph's son in very similar words: 'he is absolutely untrustworthy, as was his father before him'. He was not the first – or the last – man in public life to make such damning and damaging comparisons. When summing up Churchill's performance in his first ministerial job, at the Colonial Office, the Permanent Secretary observed that he was 'most tiresome to deal with, and will, I fear, give trouble – as his father did'. Of course, with the passage of time, there were fewer who could remember Churchill's father – but by the 1930s, everyone knew about Churchill's son. Once again, the similarities between Winston and Randolph II seemed disconcertingly close. As Sam Hoare put it in 1934: 'I do not know which is the more offensive or mischievous, Winston or his son. Rumour, however, goes that they fight like cats with each other, and chiefly agree in the prodigious amount of champagne that each of them drinks each night.'

Churchill's sense of clan loyalty extended well beyond his immediate relatives, to encompass those more distantly located on the twigs and branches of his broadly spreading family tree. One of Lord Randolph's sisters was Lady Cornelia Spencer-Churchill, who always took the greatest interest in Winston's career, 'not only for your dear father's sake, but also for you'. In 1868, she had married Ivor Guest, scion of the great dynasty of South Wales iron-masters. Guest was an incorrigible snob and social climber, whose ambitions were widely lampooned during the 1870s in the pages of *Truth* and *Vanity Fair*, so much so that he was widely known as 'the paying Guest'. He was created Baron Wimborne in 1880 by Disraeli, but turned against the Tories in the 1900s. The ostensible reason was his loyalty to Free

Trade, but a more likely explanation was rumoured to be his annoyance that his request for promotion to an earldom had been refused. In January 1910 he tried to get one of his sons, Freddie, elected for the local constituency of East Dorset in the Liberal interest. But, as was often the case when a landed family changed sides, it was claimed that the Guests exerted undue influence on their tenants, intimidating some and bribing others, and on petition the election was disallowed.

Lord Wimborne's eldest son, another Ivor Guest, was thus Churchill's first cousin. Like his father, he was a shameless importuner: Asquith thought him 'very unpopular', and the general feeling about him in social and political circles was well expressed in the damning couplet: 'One must suppose that God knew best / When he created Ivor Guest.' In 1900, he had been elected Conservative MP for Plymouth, but in 1906 he followed his father and his cousin into the Liberal Party. Actively helped by his 'friend and ally' Churchill, he sought promotion in the peerage and preferment in government. Asquith was distinctly unenthused, but in 1910 he gave Guest a peerage in his own right as Lord Ashby St Ledgers (his father was still at that time alive), and made him Paymaster-General. This did not satisfy him and, with Churchill's help, he continued to press his claims. Eventually, he accepted the Viceroyalty of Ireland in 1915, but he was not a success there, resigned three years later, consoled himself with a viscountcy, and took no further part in public life. Clementine Churchill never approved of him, and even Margot Asquith thought him 'just a fairly frank bounder'.

Ivor Guest's younger brother, Freddie, was still more

suspect. Like so many members of his family, he was a snob, a playboy and a lightweight (in 1919 he suggested that the best solution to any possible working-class unrest was to drug their tea), and he had a 'passion for begging and pushing'. He, too, left the Tories for the Liberals, but failed to get elected in 1906. Churchill thereupon appointed him one of his private secretaries, and in 1910 he became MP for the family constituency of East Dorset at the second attempt. Thanks to his cousin's efforts, minor government office soon came his way, but it was only in 1917 that he became a significant (and shadowy) political figure, when he was appointed Liberal Coalition Whip. For the next five years, Guest was responsible for raising money for Lloyd George's personal campaign fund. As a result he was closely involved in the sale of honours, and he probably set up Maundy Gregory in the touting business. During the dying months of the Coalition, he succeeded his cousin as Secretary of State for Air, but he held no office thereafter. He was completely cynical about honours, probably knew more embarrassing secrets than any other man in public life, and was regarded by Viscount Gladstone as Lloyd George's 'evil genius'. Even his *Times* obituary hinted that Freddie Guest was not a nice man to know.

Through his Marlborough grandfather's marriage to Lady Frances Anne, Churchill was also related to the Londonderry family. This was never so easy a connection as with the two Guest brothers. Between 1910 and 1914, the sixth Marquess took great exception to Churchill's championing of Irish Home Rule, and for most of the inter-war years Churchill and the seventh

Marquess were not on the best of terms. On at least two occasions, Churchill certainly put himself out for his relative: in 1919 when, as the newly appointed Secretary of State for Air, he gave him a junior job as Parliamentary Under-Secretary; and in 1928, when he successfully urged Baldwin to bring him into the Cabinet as First Commissioner of Works and Public Buildings. For much of the 1920s, however, Londonderry devoted himself to Ulster politics, a decision which Churchill thought unwise, and they did not see eye to eye over the General Strike. During the 1930s, they drifted still further apart. Churchill was a vehement critic of Londonderry while he was Secretary of State for Air, from 1931 to 1935; he disapproved of Lady Londonderry's much-publicised friendship with Ramsay MacDonald; and he found his kinsman's admiration of Adolph Hitler incomprehensible. Not surprisingly, he steadfastly refused to give Londonderry any job in his wartime coalition or caretaker Conservative administration of 1945.

The final Marlborough connection, which was also much publicised during the inter-war years, was with a cadet branch, descended from the second son of the fourth duke: the Churchills of Wychwood. The first Viscount Churchill, who had inherited the estates in 1886, sold off most of the ancestral acres and heirlooms soon after, and spent his life as a professional courtier and businessman, eventually becoming Lord-in-Waiting to King Edward VII, and chairman of the Great Western Railway. He achieved notoriety because of his long-standing and much-publicised quarrel with his wife, which effectively ruined what was left of the family's riches and reputation. Shortly before the First World War, she took up spiritualism and theosophy, under the influence of a medium named Kathleen Ellis. Lord Churchill thereupon separated from his wife, and pronounced her insane. She fled to North Africa, along with her son, and Churchill tried unsuccessfully to recapture them at gunpoint. (He eventually divorced her in a Scottish court in 1927.) During the First World War, Lady Churchill returned to Paris, set up house with Kathleen Ellis, and forced her son to marry her friend. Having already broken with his father, the son now broke with his mother, ran away to America, smoked opium, went on the stage, and was (falsely) accused of stealing the Wimborne jewels.

In addition to these more distant Marlborough relations, Churchill was also connected to another group of patrician families through his mother, Lady Randolph. Her eldest sister Clare married Moreton Frewen, the younger son of a Sussex squire, who inherited an Irish estate in the 1890s. But the man who was thus Winston's uncle mismanaged his affairs so hopelessly, and so publicly, that he was nicknamed 'Mortal Ruin'. He spent his portion of £16,000 on a cattle ranch in Wyoming, but by 1887 had lost his entire investment. Thereafter, he was involved in a variety of preposterous schemes: to make axle grease for locomotives, to produce ice artificially, to extract gold from refuse-ore, to separate lead from zinc, and to cut down timber in Kenya. (He was also responsible for correcting the proofs of Churchill's first book, and made a terrible job of it.) All these enterprises lost him borrowed money, and he was regularly on the brink of bankruptcy. His elder brother's Sussex estate was mortgaged and the timber cut down; his own Irish property was laden with debt; and he even persuaded his children to mortgage their life interests as soon as they came of age. When his daughter Clare married in 1910, it was from a house borrowed for the occasion; so bad was her father's reputation that her wedding dress had to be paid for in advance and in cash; and some of his many creditors gatecrashed the reception. At his death in 1924 he left less than £50. As Kipling put it, 'he lived in every sense except what is called common sense'.

Lady Randolph's other sister, Leonie, married Sir John Leslie, a worthy and dutiful Irish baronet, whose family owned land in County Monaghan. Their eldest son, John Randolph, was thus Winston's cousin. In one guise, he was passionately attached to the Ascendancy, and wrote a series of books lovingly recalling the lost world of his childhood. He sincerely mourned the end of the old paternalism, the demise of the great Irish estates under the Land Acts, and the suicide of European civilisation as a result of the First World War. He bitterly regretted the corrosion of high society by Jewish adventurers, and the corrupting power of the press. Yet even as he lamented the passing of his patrician heritage, he also deliberately rejected it. He 'deeply affronted the Anglo-Irish Ascendancy into which he had been born', by renouncing his right of succession to the family estates, by embracing Roman Catholicism, and by using Shane, the Irish form of his name. Even more to his relatives' dismay, he took up the cause of Irish Nationalism and, thanks to Churchill's intercession, was introduced to John Redmond. In January 1910, he contested Londonderry City as an Irish Nationalist, standing against the heir to the ducal house of Abercorn, and in 1916, he urged that the British government should not execute those who had taken part in the Easter Rising. He was, in short, an authentically maverick patrician.

Lady Randolph's remarkable matrimonial career brought two more tainted notables into Churchill's family orbit. One of them was her second husband, George Cornwallis-West. He was the heir to Ruthin Castle in Denbighshire, one of the oldest estates on the Welsh borders. By the late nineteenth century it was sadly decayed, and his parents were very short of money. Under these circumstances, marrying the spendthrift Lady Randolph was an extremely imprudent move, and by 1906 Cornwallis-West's finances were so precarious that Churchill was obliged to come to his step-father's assistance. In order to make some urgently needed money, he mortgaged his reversionary interest in the Ruthin estates, and – against the characteristically shrewd advice of Sir Ernest Cassel – set up a small issuing house in the City. Then everything went wrong. In 1914 he divorced Lady Randolph and married Mrs Patrick Campbell. In 1916 his business collapsed and he was declared bankrupt. And in 1920 he had to sell the family estates, to which he had succeeded three years before, to discharge his debts. Meanwhile, his marriage to Mrs Pat had broken down, he found it impossible to obtain a job in the inter-war years, and he was obliged to eke out a living writing reminiscences, novels and biographies. Mrs Campbell refused to grant him a divorce, and it was only on her death in 1940 that he was able to marry again. Shortly afterwards, he contracted Parkinson's disease, and he committed suicide in 1951.

Through his step-father's sister, Constance Cornwallis-West, Churchill's family ties were strengthened with another flawed and fallen grandee: Bend Or, second Duke of Westminster. The Marlboroughs and the Grosvenors were already twice connected, via the Guests, and in 1901 Constance became the first of Bend Or's wives. The Cornwallis-Wests hoped thereby to repair their own family fortunes, but the marriage was not a success. The son and heir the duchess bore her husband died in 1909, and thereafter the couple went their separate ways. In 1919 they were divorced, amidst much adverse publicity, and three more marriages brought Bend Or neither happiness nor repose. He was obliged to resign the Lord Lieutenancy of Cheshire because of his matrimonial irregularities, and neither King George V nor King George VI would have anything to do with him. This social ostracism only intensified his restless paranoia. He hated democracy, disliked Jews, voted against the Parliament Bill in 1910, and favoured a negotiated peace with Hitler. On his death in 1953, Henry Channon composed a damning epitaph: 'he was restless, spoilt, irritable . . . ; his life was an empty failure . . . ; he did few kindnesses, leaves no monument'. Churchill had always felt rather differently, and issued a statement from 10 Downing Street, looking back 'affectionately and thankfully over half a century of unbroken friendship'.

Clementine's aristocratic relatives were at least as unrespectable as those of her mother-in-law. Her sister, Nellie, who gambled and was generally considered rather 'fast', married Bertram Romilly, whose forebears were of illustrious lineage, but not rich. (Indeed, for a time in the 1920s, Nellie was obliged to keep a hat shop to help make ends meet.) There were two children of their marriage, Esmond and Giles, who were thus Winston's nephews, and they regularly visited Chartwell during the inter-war years. In 1934, Esmond became newsworthy in a sensational manner, by running away from Wellington College. He declared himself a Communist, and began to produce a subversive periodical entitled *Out of Bounds*. Inevitably, the press had a field day, publishing sensational stories under such unfortunate but predictable headlines as 'Winston's Red Nephew'. To make matters worse, Esmond possessed both a Churchillian countenance and a Churchillian temperament, and it was widely rumoured that he was in fact Winston's illegitimate son. For the rest of the decade, he remained constantly in the news. In 1936, he went to Spain, and fought on the side of the pro-Republican forces. In the following year, in an even greater blaze of publicity, he eloped with his cousin, Jessica Mitford.

This was not the only connection between Clementine Churchill and the Mitfords. Her aunt, Clementina Ogilvy, had married Bertram Mitford, first Baron Redesdale. (Indeed, it was whispered in some quarters that Bertram was in fact Clementine's father.) As a result, the Mitford children were frequent visitors to Chartwell, and Randolph showed a more than fleeting interest in Diana. By the 1930s the family was in serious financial trouble, and four of the daughters were regularly hitting the headlines: Nancy embraced socialism, and began writing novels; Jessica preferred communism and ran away with

Esmond Romilly; Unity became a wholehearted supporter of Hitler; and Diana, having divorced Bryan Guinness, married Sir Oswald Mosley. Once again, Churchill suffered because of these distant but definite connections. In the late 1930s, both the English and the German press made much of the fact that Winston and Unity were relatives. And it was more than mildly embarrassing to the new wartime Prime Minister that two of the first people to be interned under the Defence of the Realm Regulations in 1940 were Sir Oswald and Lady Mosley. (It was even rumoured that the same fate had befallen Lord Londonderry.)

Of course, these were not the only relatives on Churchill's extended aristocratic family tree. Some were worthy public men, like his uncle, Lord Tweedmouth, who was Lord President of the Council in Asquith's administration (though he did go insane and had to resign). Others lived lives of unostentatious decency, like his aunt, Lady Anne Spencer-Churchill, who married the seventh Duke of Roxburghe, and was Mistress of the Robes to Queen Victoria. But these were not the relations who hit the headlines, or who became the subject of malicious gossip and rumour. By contrast, and by definition, those who did were invariably good copy, and, as with his more immediate relatives, these disreputable family connections can only have done Churchill harm in the eyes of the politicians and the public. In November 1915 Moreton Frewen wrote to every member of Asquith's Cabinet, urging that Churchill should not be allowed to resign in the aftermath of the Dardanelles (his letter was ignored). In September 1939, by which time he was working as a journalist, Esmond Romilly urged that his uncle be made Prime Minister. It is difficult to believe this did his cause much help.

At the very least, Churchill's vigorous loyalty to his more distant kinsmen was regarded by his fellow politicians as 'tiresome' and 'inconsiderate'. He was too persistent and too unsubtle an intriguer, and some of his efforts were clearly counter-productive. More damningly, the fact that he took great trouble to promote the political careers of such suspect patrician lightweights as the Guest brothers or Lord Londonderry can only have reinforced the widely held view that his behaviour was nepotistic, and his judgement was suspect. And it is difficult to imagine what he must have been thinking of when, at the Westminster by-election of 1924, he took with him on his campaign what Robert Rhodes James tactfully describes as 'a somewhat variegated assemblage of allies', including such déclassés and mavericks as Moreton Frewen, Freddie Guest, Shane Leslie and the Duke of Marlborough. Such ostentatiously flaunted associations, even if based on the admirable view that blood was thicker than water, were exceptionally ill-advised.

Viewed from this essentially dynastic perspective, Churchill's reputation may best be described as genealogically precarious, and it is in this unsavoury familial context of widespread degeneracy and disreputability that his own finances, friends, and way of life must be set and understood. As the elder son of a younger son, Churchill's inherited wealth was likely to be insubstantial, but because of his father's profligacy it was virtually non-existent. At his death, Lord Randolph's assets almost exactly matched his liabilities, and Winston himself was left to subsist as best he could on an allowance of £500 a year. To make matters worse, his mother was a spendthrift, with no real understanding of the value of money, his marriage to Clementine brought him no financial advantage (quite the reverse), and from his earliest years in the army Churchill believed that he had a right to the most comfortable and indulgent style of life. As a result, his own finances, while never as desparate as those of Moreton Frewen or George Cornwallis-West, were for most of his life decidedly uncertain. From the 1890s until the Second World War, he seems almost never to have been out of debt. Even (indeed especially) for a man of Churchill's aristocratic self-confidence, this was a precarious base from which to launch what soon became a flamboyant and controversial political career.

It was Churchill's proud boast on New Year's Day 1901 that in less than two years he had made £10,000 by his own unaided efforts, from his journalism, his lectures and his books. In this he was quite correct, and to that extent his claim to be a self-made man was entirely justified. By then, his need for capital (and income) had for some time been self-evident. As a cadet at Sandhurst he had been continually short of money, and soon got into debt, and he experienced the greatest difficulty in finding the £650 necessary for equipping himself for the Fourth Hussars in 1895. The Dowager Duchess Lily gave him a charger worth £200, and he borrowed the rest of the money from the bank. Two years later, in India, his combined allowance and income amounted to only £800 a year, he was obliged to resort to local and unscrupulous money-lenders, and some of his cheques were dishonoured (a much more serious offence against the gentlemanly code of conduct then than now). Meanwhile, his mother spent and squandered as if there would be no tomorrow. 'We are,' Churchill remonstrated with her in 1898, 'both you and I, equally thoughtless, spendthrift and extravagant. . . . We are damned poor.'

Nor did his turn-of-the-century success as an author, journalist and lecturer improve his financial condition for long. In 1899, when he resigned his commission, he lost his only regular income. Two years later he voluntarily made over to his mother the £500-a-year allowance due from his father's estate. Once he was launched into the costly world of early twentieth-century politics, Churchill's financial position became even more precarious. At that time, MPs received no remuneration, and were further expected to contribute to their own election expenses. Churchill was helped out by the Duke of Marlborough (who also provided him with lodgings in London), and subsequently by the Wimbornes. By 1906, his capital was much diminished. Like his father, he needed an official salary (indeed, there were some who accused him of crossing the floor for this very reason). Like his father, again, he soon sought the society and support of rich financiers, in particular Lord Randolph's old friend, Sir Ernest Cassel. It was not just that Churchill put the management of his £10,000 in Cassel's capable hands; it was also that Cassel found Jack Churchill a job as a stockbroker, and even put some directorships in the way of George Cornwallis-West.

Inevitably, Churchill's marriage to the impecunious

Clementine, his rapidly growing family, and his meteoric promotion in government, only increased his financial burdens. By 1910 his official salary was a welcome £2,500, but his outgoings were much more than that. Like his father, he was obliged to rely on the largesse of others. Sir Ernest Cassel paid for the furnishings of Churchill's drawing-room 'as an act of spontaneous friendship', and Mrs Keppel (who was, after all, well placed to know) once suggested to Clementine that she could best help her husband's career by taking a rich and well-placed lover. In 1913 it was rumoured that Churchill had speculated in Marconi shares, and by the outbreak of war he was obliged to admit that 'our finances are in a condition which requires serious and prompt attention. . . . Money seems to flow away.' Indeed, at one point the position was so bleak that Clementine was forced to sell a necklace to pay the household expenses. By the time Churchill departed for active service on the Western Front, the loss of his official salary, combined with his accumulated debts, meant he was effectively dependent on the 'unlimited credit' of Sir Ernest Cassel. Had her husband been killed in the trenches, Clementine would have been left with less than £1,000 a year.

Although Cassel was both a financial genius and a genuine friend, Churchill's dependence on him did not enhance his own political reputation. For Cassel was widely disliked and distrusted as a 'cosmopolitan financier', whose loyalty was neither to party nor to nation, but only to profits. As a German, a Jew, a millionaire, and a friend of King Edward VII, he seemed a classic example of the unscrupulous and unpatriotic plutocrat who was disfiguring public life, an irresponsible wire-puller who had poor politicians in his pocket. In 1902, Lord Salisbury had refused the King's request that Cassel should be made a peer, and during the First World War he was the subject of much hostile criticism on account of his alien origins. In 1922, Lord Alfred Douglas stated publicly that Churchill was Cassel's creature: that 'this ambitious and brilliant man, short of money and eager for power', had given a deliberately false account of the Battle of Jutland, in exchange for a large sum of money. Douglas was prosecuted for criminal libel, convicted, and sent to prison. But in the course of the trial it emerged that Cassel had indeed paid for Churchill's drawing-room – a gift which, in the climate of the times, he had probably been unwise to accept. Although Churchill won his case, gossip about his unsound financial affairs was never fully silenced.

At almost exactly the same time, Churchill acquired Chartwell Manor, the house which, after Blenheim, he loved the most in all his life. In theory, it was paid for by an unexpected legacy he had received in 1922 from the settlement of his Londonderry grandmother, Frances Anne, combined with an early advance for *The World Crisis*. But from the very beginning its upkeep was a drain on Churchill's meagre resources. To the initial cost of £5,000 was soon added £15,000-worth of improvements. There was an indoor and outdoor staff of eighteen to maintain; and there were costly and unsuccessful attempts to rear cattle, sheep, pigs and hens. By 1926, even Churchill admitted the need to economise: the livestock was sold off, spending was curtailed, and there was even talk of letting the house. But extravagance kept breaking out, and Churchill stubbornly refused to moderate his expensive way of life. Servants, he breezily insisted, were there to save trouble, and should be hired and fired with ease. Not surprisingly, Clementine took a less serene view, and her worst forebodings were realised when, in the crash of 1929, Churchill lost most of his American investments.

Throughout the 1930s, Churchill's finances were in a truly parlous condition. Chartwell continued to absorb money like a sponge, and this, combined with the expenses associated with his children (in particular their education and the payment of their debts) meant that by 1931 his overdraft stood at £9,500. Seven years later a renewed slump on Wall Street left him owing his brokers £18,000. Stringent economy measures were again introduced, but his creditors were so pressing that Churchill felt compelled to put Chartwell on the market, and even thought of quitting public life altogether. Eventually, his house and his career were saved by the generosity of Sir Henry Strakosch, an Austrian-born financier and South African mining magnate, who took responsibility for all his debts, and guaranteed to pay the interest on them. *Pace* David Irving, this does not mean that Churchill was the creature of an international conspiracy of Jewish money-lenders. Indeed, the exact details of Strakosch's intervention remained secret for many years. But it was widely known that Churchill did not seem able to manage his own finances, and at the time when he was seeking to rouse parliament and the nation to the Nazi threat this must have been a political liability, as well as a grave personal anxiety.

In the same way, Churchill's obvious – and under-standable – delight in living well at someone else's expense did not do him any good in the more strait-laced political circles. During the 1900s, he regularly holidayed with Sir Ernest Cassel: in Spain, on Nile cruises, and at his villa in Switzerland. He also enjoyed the equally lavish hospitality of Baron de Forest, both in London and at his estate in Austria. And one of the great attractions for Churchill of being First Lord of the Admiralty, and later Chancellor of the Exchequer, was that the job carried with it an official residence in London. As First Lord he also had at his disposal the Admiralty yacht, *Enchantress*, which he used as a float-ing hotel, to entertain officially, to reciprocate the hospi-tality of his plutocratic friends, and to cosset his family. It cost Churchill 'nothing or next to nothing', and the fact that such high living was paid for by the state was the subject of much adverse comment at the time. 'How many lobsters have been eaten?' inquired Leo Maxse in the *National Review*. 'How many magnums of cham-pagne have been drunk? To say nothing of other deli-cacies comprising a democratic diet.' Churchill was impervious to such criticisms of his subsidised high living. Indeed, for much of the First World War, he was provided with the use of a Rolls-Royce by his friend the second Duke of Westminster.

During the inter-war years, he remained a shameless cadger and incorrigible scrounger. When he visited the United States, in 1929 and again in 1931, he invariably travelled in private railcars, provided by such rich friends as the financier Bernard Baruch and the steel magnate Charles Schwab. In California he was accommodated by William Randolph Hearst at San Simeon, and when he and Randolph put up at the Biltmore Hotel in Los Angeles their suite was paid for by James Rathwell Page, appropriately described by Churchill as 'a hearty banker'. In France, Winston and Clementine regularly stayed at the houses of the Duke of Westminster and Consuelo Balsan, the former Duchess of Marlborough, who had subsequently married a rich Frenchman. Churchill, though not his wife, also loved the French Riviera, and frequently wrote and painted while staying at the villas of Lord Beaverbrook, Lord Rothermere, and Maxine Elliott, the American socialite. Subsidised yachting also remained a favourite pastime. As devotees of Noel Coward will know, the Duke of Westminster owned two magnificent vessels, on which the Churchills frequently cruised. Walter Guinness, Lord Moyne, was equally hospitable: in 1934 the Churchills were taken on an extended cruise of the eastern Mediterranean in his yacht, the *Rosaura*, and in the following year Clementine again sailed with Moyne on a six-month journey to the Dutch East Indies.

As these names suggest, Churchill's friends were almost invariably drawn from the raffish worlds of high politics and high finance. His close collaboration with Lloyd George lasted from 1906 until 1922: first as his ally in radical, peer-bashing reform, then as his colleague in a coalition widely regarded as the most corrupt and irresponsible government of the twentieth century. Either way, this did not endear Churchill to the moralising politicians who dominated British public life from 1922 to 1939. The fact that Churchill had defended Lloyd George at the time of the Marconi Scandal was not soon forgotten. It was rumoured that the reason why Lloyd George had braved Tory wrath in bringing Churchill back into the government in 1917 as Minister of Munitions was that he was 'able to blackmail the Prime Minister'. There is no evidence that Churchill was ever involved personally in the sale of honours; but Freddie Guest was, after all, his cousin, and Churchill himself was a regular attender at the Derby dinners arranged by Maundy Gregory at the Ambassadors Club during the 1920s.

Nor did Churchill's much-advertised and much-celebrated admiration for Lord Birkenhead exactly enhance his reputation as a man of probity and good judgement. They first met in 1906, soon after F. E. Smith (as Birkenhead then was) had made his brilliant maiden speech in the Commons. Together they founded the Other Club, they served in the Lloyd George Coalition from 1917 to 1922, and Churchill never ceased to regard him as his greatest and most gifted friend. Although he was a brilliant barrister, Birkenhead was a drunk, a gambler and a spendthrift, who shamelessly pursued the glittering prizes of life, and treated anyone who got in his way with an unforgivable (and unforgettable) combination of rudeness and ruthlessness. He was a close friend of Maundy Gregory, by whom it was rumoured he was being blackmailed, and he was forced to leave politics in 1928 because his creditors would not wait. Lord Balcarres described him as a man with 'the spirit and sometimes the ethics of a freebooter'. Lord Salisbury was even more censorious: 'I do not imagine', he once observed, 'that he has got many political principles. Poor fellow, he will probably drink himself to death.' And so, in the end, he did.

Lord Beaverbrook possessed greater staying power, and his friendship with Churchill lasted from before the First World War until the end of their days. For most of his life, Beaverbrook was regarded – with good reason – as an unscrupulous adventurer and a mischief-maker. He was a self-made Canadian businessman, who arrived in England in 1910, and in quick succession became an MP, a knight, a baronet and a peer. Asquith was not alone in believing that Beaverbrook's Canadian business record was 'of the shadiest', and his rapid accumulation of honours provoked 'a howl of indignation and disgust' in his home country. In 1916 he acquired the *Daily Express*, and by the inter-war years he was one of the most powerful press barons in the land. In addition to Churchill, his close friends included Lloyd George, Bonar Law and Birkenhead, and all of them benefited from his hospitality or financial assistance. The result was that Beaverbrook seemed to wield influence which was both sinister and irresponsible: propelling Law to the Conservative leadership in 1911; bringing down the Asquith government in December 1916; and destroying the Lloyd George Coalition in 1922. By then, indeed, he was widely regarded as the embodiment of all the evil forces which threatened to corrupt British public life.

Very much the same was said of Brendan Bracken, who first met Churchill in 1923, and became, by the 1930s, his most stalwart public and parliamentary friend. Bracken was a mysterious Irish hustler, a whole generation younger than Churchill or Beaverbrook, who established himself as the dominant figure in financial journalism in the inter-war years, and became MP for Paddington in 1929. His devotion to Churchill was total:

he helped to place his articles in newspapers, and it was thanks to his initiative that Henry Strakosch came to Churchill's financial rescue in 1938. This was, however, another friendship which did Churchill's public standing considerable harm. Bracken was generally regarded as being a brash, pushy, meretricious, over-familiar and disrespectful opportunist; and it was widely believed (even in the Churchill family itself) that he was Winston's illegitimate child. With characteristic indifference, Churchill himself was amused and slightly flattered by such rumours, but Clementine was understandably enraged at these aspersions on her husband's integrity, and damningly dismissed Bracken as a 'red-haired freak'.

Although, as a life-long Liberal, Clementine retained a sneaking admiration for Lloyd George, she greatly disapproved of Birkenhead, Beaverbrook and Bracken, whom she labelled the 'three terrible Bs'. She knew that in their roistering, buccaneering company Churchill drank and gambled to excess. She feared that they brought out all that was worst in her husband: his irresponsibility, his belligerence and his waywardness. She was convinced that his widely known delight in the friendship of three such piratical adventurers only damaged his public standing. After all, no one could accuse Churchill of having chosen his disreputable relatives: that was a matter over which by definition he had no control. But in selecting his friends, he showed personal preferences for men equally unsavoury. The least that could be said was that he had been impelled by temperament, by fallible judgement, and by financial necessity to seek wealthy, untrustworthy and unreliable associates which a more careful and more prudent politician would have taken pains to avoid. More damagingly, it bore out the truth of Brendan Bracken's remark, that Churchill too easily gathered charlatans around him – of whom many believed Bracken himself to be one.

These unwise and much-publicised friendships, combined with the broader family background of ducal degeneracy, help to explain why it was so easy for critics to disparage Churchill's conduct and character for so much of his career. Moreover, his own behaviour and way of life only seemed to confirm this hostile view. From the day he escaped from prison in the Boer War, there were regular rumours that he had broken his parole, which repeated libel actions never fully laid to rest. At different times, it was put about that his brother was not his brother, and that he had fathered two illegitimate children. Like his father, and his own children, he ate, drank, gambled and spent to excess. He showed no respect for religious belief or spiritual values, and his conversation was often Rabelaisian. His finances were known to be unsound, and there were rumours and accusations that he was the client of rich and dangerous men. In 1940, for instance, the Aga Khan claimed that 'for years' Churchill had been in the pay of the Jews and Lord Beaverbrook. At the very least, it seemed as though Churchill had inherited more than his fair share of Marlborough delinquency and instability.

The whispering and the accusations went further than that, for it was even suggested that Churchill's wayward and erratic behaviour was evidence that his father's syphilis had been congenital. In 1925, Frank Harris published his memoirs, which gave a gruesome and fanciful account of Lord Randolph's terminal insanity. The book was banned in England; but copies certainly made their way into the country, and can only have fed the fires of rumour. All this, combined with Churchill's known liking for alcohol, and his increased consumption in his ten years out of office, made it easy for the official Conservative leadership to launch a whispering campaign against his character and capabilities during the 1930s. Of course, this was a maliciously exaggerated picture, but it must have done Churchill untold damage. For there was ample material available from which to paint it; and the image stuck. In the spring of 1940, when Churchill became Prime Minister, one of the greatest concerns in official circles, in Whitehall, and in Washington, was that he would not be up to the job because he was a drunk.

Unlike many needy notables of the time, Churchill did not get into debt because he would not (or could not) earn a living, but because the very substantial sums which he did pull in were never enough for his indulgent needs. By 1900, he had already resolved that he would support himself by his pen, and 54 years later he could proudly claim that was the only means by which he had ever earned his living. Even for a full-time writer, Churchill's output would have been remarkable. For a man whose main career was politics and government, it was quite extraordinary. By 1914, he had already published four books based on his early adventures, a two-volume biography of his father, several political pamphlets, a collection of his speeches, and one novel. Between the wars, he produced *The World Crisis* in six volumes, his life of Marlborough in four, his own auto-biography, and four more books of occasional essays and speeches. They paid astonishingly well. From Macmillan, Churchill received an advance of £8,000 for his life of Lord Randolph. For his biography of Marlborough, Walter Harrap paid £10,000, and Charles Scribner another £5,000 for the American rights. And Cassell's initial advance for his *History of the English-Speaking Peoples* was £20,000.

Like so much of his life before 1940, Churchill's literary output needs to be set in the broader context of aristocratic activity and decline. From the 1880s to the 1930s there was a marked increase in the number of notables who were publishing books about themselves and their families. Some, like Lord Willoughby de Broke, Lady Londonderry, the Duke of Portland and Lady Fingall, wrote autobiographies which nostalgically recalled the vanished world of their youth. Some published extended editions of family correspondence, like the Earl of Ilchester on the Foxes and Holland House, and Nancy Mitford on the Stanleys of Alderley. Some produced books about dynasties and mansions: Vita Sackville-West on Knole and the Sackvilles, and Lord Lansdowne on Glanerought and the Petty-Fitzmaurices. Some wrote multi-volume biographies of their relatives: Lord Crewe on Lord Rosebery, Lady Blanche Dugdale on A. J. Balfour, and Lady Gwendolen Cecil on Lord Salisbury. However varied the quality of these works (they were memorably parodied by Nancy Mitford in the opening pages of *The Pursuit of Love*), they all shared one unstated assumption: in their pious celebration of family greatness, they implicitly recognised that the unchallenged dominion of the traditional governing classes was now becoming a thing of the past.

Much of Churchill's formidable output was clearly derived from these readily available models of aristocratic literary endeavour. His one explicit venture into auto-biography, *My Early Life*, was a classic piece of patrician reminiscence, in more senses than one. Its agreeably self-deprecating tone, its wit and its warmth, its pace and its zest, mark it out from most run-of-the-mill productions. But in most respects, it was a recognisable example of the genre: a nostalgic re-creation of a vanished youthful world, in which a series of predictable episodes and experiences were recounted. There were early recollec-tions – of life in the big house, of parents and relatives, of nannies and servants. There were descriptions of school days – of teachers (good and bad), of lessons (mostly unsuccessful) and of games (where the results were rather better). There was an account of entry into Sandhurst, of training for the army, and of the first commission. There were adventures in plenty – war service in Cuba, India, the Sudan and South Africa. There was the begin-ning of a political career: the early attempts at public speaking, the first battles at the hustings, the successful election to parliament, and the maiden speech.

Churchill's biography of Lord Randolph also followed a standard format: the two-volume life, suffused by a powerful sense of family piety and ancestral veneration. It was dedicated to the ninth Duke of Marlborough 'in all faithful friendship', and opens with a magniloquent description of Blenheim and its park, so *fortissimo* and *noblimente* as to be almost overwhelming in its rhetorical luxuriance. As with most aristocratic productions of that type, too much space was given over to the extended printing of original letters and documents, so that in many places the author did little more than provide a commentary on the correspondence. As was also customary, Churchill admiringly and uncritically depicted his father as a public paragon. The many private and temperamental shortcomings were ignored, the evidence was carefully adjusted where needs be, the political triumphs were appropriately celebrated, and the eventual failure was transformed into something akin to a Greek tragedy. Except that in this case, Churchill insisted, it was Lord Randolph's virtues which proved his undoing, for he was too consistent for his own good. Having been rejected by the Tories, Winston clearly implied, his father should have gone over to the Liberals. But that was something he was too high-minded to do.

By thus depicting Lord Randolph as a far-sighted, unswerving, high-principled statesman, Churchill was determined to refute the unflattering image of his father – as a déclassé opportunist and inconsistent adventurer – which still prevailed in political and social circles in the 1900s, only ten years after his death. (How far he succeeded in this is not at all clear: most reviews were favourable, but those who had known Lord Randolph were privately less convinced.) Yet there was more to this exercise in sanitised rehabilitation than the dictates of family piety, strong though that motive undoubtedly was. In his early years in politics, Churchill constantly sought to attract attention by modelling himself on Lord Randolph. But while he wanted to be thought of as embodying his father's virtues, many had reached the parallel conclusion, that he possessed all his father's faults. It was thus of supreme importance for him to project in his biography an image of Lord Randolph that was wholesome and admirable, an imaginative portrayal of 'the best side' of his father which was also deliberately designed to serve Churchill's more immediate political needs. For by arguing that Lord Randolph's supreme tragedy was that he did not join the Liberals, having fallen out with the Tories, Winston provided a carefully worked-out defence of his own recent political conduct in crossing the floor.

In his much-larger-scale biography of the first Duke of Marlborough, the theme of family piety was even stronger. Churchill undertook the work as 'a duty', and the ninth Duke kept the Blenheim archive closed until he and his research assistants could work on it. Once again large parts of the resulting volumes consisted of massive extracts from original documents, sometimes ill-digested, and often unnecessarily lengthy. Once again, Churchill conceived this work as an enterprise in advocacy and atonement. For his aim was to destroy the 'odious portrait' which 'a long succession of the most famous writers in the English language' had painted. Instead of Macaulay's unscrupulous adventurer, who changed sides, who loved power, and who loved money, Churchill used all his rhetorical skills to depict Marlborough as a patriotic hero, a 'virtuous and benevolent being', a victorious and magnanimous warrior, and a European statesman of the first rank who was loved by his soldiers, trusted by his allies, and respected even by his enemies. In thus pointing the contrast between 'the glory and importance of his deeds, and the small regard of his countrymen for his memory', Churchill hoped to win for his hero 'a more just and more generous judgement from his fellow countrymen'.

As with his biography of Lord Randolph, Churchill's life of Marlborough was a two-way dialogue with his forebears: but very much on his own terms. It was timely to remind the world of the past glories of his family, in a decade, the 1930s, when they seemed distinctly faded. Once again, the charges levelled at the great duke – his opportunism, his unreliability, his love of money, his craving for power – had often been levelled, not only at Lord Randolph, but at Winston, too. As Henry Steele Commager has rightly pointed out, Churchill's 'vindication of Marlborough from neglect and contumely was, in a sense, a vindication of himself'. And just as the biography of Lord Randolph had legitimised Churchill's change of political party in the 1900s, so his life of Marlborough, depicting the embattled hero surrounded by snarling and sniping politicians, provided ancestral validation for his beleaguered stand against appeasement in the 1930s. The historical parallels were very close, and for Churchill were very real. But not everyone was persuaded. In October 1938, he delivered one of his most powerful speeches, against the Munich agreement, yet the *Daily Express* contemptuously dismissed it as 'an alarmist oration by a man whose mind is soaked in the conquests of Marlborough'.

Churchill's autobiography and works of ancestral piety belonged to a recognisable genre of contemporary aristocratic writing, and the same was true of his journalism. For the revolution in newspaper production during the last quarter of the nineteenth century coincided with the decline in aristocratic incomes as a consequence of the agricultural depression, and in this changed financial climate many straitened notables took to writing for the press. Some were entirely serious, like Lord Montagu of Beaulieu, proprietor of *Car Illustrated* and later motoring correspondent for *The Times*. Some were less respectable, like the Countess of Warwick, or Churchill's mother, who wrote a series of articles for *Pearson's Magazine* during the First World War on such inconsequential subjects as 'The Girl of Today', 'Friendship' and 'Extravagance' (she certainly knew something about that). Some, trading on their good connections, became gossip columnists, like Lords Castlerosse and Donegall (and also, during the 1930s, Randolph Churchill, who maintained a long-running and much-publicised feud with Castlerosse.) These déclassés were greatly disapproved of by high-minded grandees like Lord Crawford, who saw in them the ultimate sign of aristocratic degeneracy. In more senses than one, writing for the papers had become a common patrician pastime.

From the 1890s until the 1930s, Churchill was closely involved in this journalistic world. Initially, as a soldier of fortune, he wrote for the press as a war correspondent. By the 1920s his work was appearing regularly in British newspapers, and was widely syndicated in the United States and continental Europe. Much of Churchill's interwar journalism was of a very high quality: in particular his reviews of biographies and his essays on political affairs, some of which were later republished as *Great Contemporaries* and *Thoughts and Adventures*. Not surprisingly, his pen was sought after by most of the great proprietors, including Hearst, Beaverbrook, Rothermere and Camrose, and they all paid him handsomely. In 1930 he signed a ten-year contract with *Collier's*, and undertook to produce six articles annually for £2,000. In 1931, the *Daily Mail* agreed to pay him £7,800 if he wrote a weekly article for twelve months, and he earned another £2,400 from the *Sunday Pictorial* for twelve essays on 'British personalities'. Together with the advances on his books, it was these lucrative newspaper contracts which provided Churchill with his main source of income. Like many an impoverished aristocrat, he was driven to write for the papers by sheer financial necessity.

Inevitably, this meant that many of the four hundred-odd articles that he churned out during the 1930s were little more than pot-boilers. For American readers, he dashed off pieces on 'Depression', 'Iced water', and 'Corn on the cob'. For his British audience, he wrote on 'Premiers on the sick list', 'How we carry liquor', 'I was astonished by Morocco', and 'Have you a hobby?' In 1931 he was run over in New York, and promptly described his misadventures in two articles for the *Daily Mail*, which earned him £600. In the following year he agreed to retell 'Twelve great stories of the world', for the *Chicago Tribune* and the *News of the World*. They were largely prepared by Eddie Marsh and included *Don Quixote, Uncle Tom's Cabin*, and *Ben Hur*. In the same vein, he later summarised *War and Peace* for the *New York News* for $1,000. On occasions, Churchill was so hard pressed for time and for money that he even recycled his own work. *My Early Life* was published in 1930. Five years later, Churchill produced twelve pieces for the *News of the World*, entitled 'My Life'. And in 1937-8 he cobbled together ten more essays on 'My life and times', for the *Sunday Chronicle*.

This steady outpouring of journalistic ephemera cannot have enhanced Churchill's reputation. Although recognising that it was financially necessary, Clementine constantly regretted that he wrote for the papers, and was convinced that 'unworthy or unsuitable contracts for "pot-boiling" newspaper and magazine articles' trivialised his standing in the public eye. (It certainly did so in the cases of Lord Birkenhead, Lloyd George and Ramsay Macdonald, the other politicians who regularly appeared in the press.) There can be no doubt that his financial dependence on the press barons – those inter-war harlots, who craved power without responsibility, and were heartily despised by all decent folk – only reinforced the view that Churchill was beholden to the most unsavoury and mischievous elements in public life. It can hardly have seemed coincidence that Rothermere contributed to Randolph's election expenses at Wavertree, or that Beaverbrook and Churchill were in alliance at the time of the Abdication. There is no reason to think that any of the press barons directly influenced Churchill's political views, but his independence and integrity must have seemed compromised by his close association with these disreputable men.

Like so much else about him, Churchill's literary endeavours – whether his journalistic pot-boilers or his multi-volume excursions into family piety – were a larger-than-life version of a commonplace aristocratic practice. But for all the money which they realised, there was also a price to be paid. As an historian and biographer, it is not at all clear that Churchill succeeded in his self-appointed role as guardian of the family flame. Theodore Roosevelt dismissed his book on his father as 'a clever, tactful, and rather cheap and vulgar life of that clever, tactful, and rather cheap and vulgar egoist'. And Churchill's attempt to rehabilitate Marlborough by traducing Macaulay provoked a magisterial rebuke from G. M. Trevelyan. Even more unfortunately, he was compelled to spend so much time on his books and his journalism that he spent less time on public affairs than was wise. During the 1930s, Churchill hardly ever attended the Commons except to make a speech, and this certainly did his reputation harm, and diminished his political appeal and effectiveness. Indeed, by the very end of the decade, he was so hard pressed for his publisher's final advance of £7,500 that he continued to work on his *History of the English-Speaking Peoples* throughout his time as First Lord of the Admiralty, even when the Norwegian campaign was at its height.

The last aspect of Churchill's ambiguous aristocratic inheritance that must be considered is its impact on his political activity and his political outlook. As Sir John Plumb has explained, Churchill's view of the world, and of his own place within it, was essentially conditioned by a strong but crude attitude towards the past: the Whig interpretation of history which the British upper classes had evolved to explain (and justify) themselves and their pre-eminence, a myth in which Churchill believed with all the unquestioning certainty of a religious creed. To him, British history was the saga of the nation's gradual, providential rise to greatness, guided by the firm but benevolent hand of an enlightened ruling aristocracy. Limited monarchy, parliamentary government, liberty and property, expanding overseas dominion: this was the picture of the British Empire, the British constitution and British society which Churchill absorbed during those formative years at the close of the nineteenth century. How, in the light of this essentially aristocratic outlook, did he react to the first forty years of the twentieth century, when events increasingly conspired to question, rather than to affirm, this serene patrician view?

If his biography of his father was to be believed, it was an easy and natural step from Tory Democracy, as preached by Lord Randolph, to a broader belief in Liberal social reforms, and from 1908 to 1911 Churchill zealously devoted himself to this cause. All his efforts on behalf of the poor – regulating wages and conditions in the mines and the sweated trades, and setting up labour exchanges and unemployment insurance – were essentially authoritarian and paternalistic in their benevolence. As Lord Crawford later remarked, the whole tenor of Churchill's mind was 'anti-radical'. For all his 'discovery of the poor', his social vision remained fundamentally aristocratic: of a benign but hierarchical society, in which the natural order was strengthened, not subverted, by social reform. As Lady Violet Bonham Carter observed, 'Lloyd George was saturated with class consciousness; but Winston accepted class distinction without a thought.' Or, as C. F. G. Masterman put it, 'He desired in England a state of things where a benign upper class dispensed benefits to an industrious, *bien pensant*, and grateful working class.' In 1942 Herbert Morrison made precisely the same point, describing Churchill as 'the old, benevolent, Tory squire, who does all he can for the people – provided they are good, obedient people, and loyally recognise his position, and theirs'.

Having left the Tories for the Liberals between 1904 and 1906, Churchill was widely believed to have committed the ultimate act of class disloyalty, of social apostasy. His performance during the debates over the People's Budget and the House of Lords crisis did nothing to dispel this view, for his language was almost as violent as that of Lloyd George himself. 'The upkeep of aristocracy', he observed, in a memorable retort to Lord Curzon, 'has been the hard work of all civilisations.' He dismissed the House of Lords as 'an institution absolutely foreign to the spirit of the age and the whole movement of society', which was 'one-sided, hereditary, unpurged, unrepresentative, irresponsible, absentee'. Indeed, in his most extreme moments, he seemed prepared to contemplate the total abolition of the House of Lords, and even the break-up of the system of great estates. Yet this was a man who weekended at Blenheim and worked to advance the careers of his titled relatives! To many Liberals, it merely betokened a lack of sincere commitment; to many Conservatives, it was the predictably squalid action of Lord Randolph's appropriately opportunist son. Either way, Churchill never seems to have realised that, by agitating the language of class war so vigorously, he was in danger of destabilising that very paternal and aristocratic society which at heart he so loved and so unthinkingly accepted.

By the inter-war years, this realisation had finally struck home, and Churchill became 'deeply disturbed by the collapse of settled values and ancient institutions'. Much of his writing in this period was suffused with the commonplace patrician nostalgia for the lost Eden of great estates, great families, and 'the old, spacious country-house life'. In *The World Crisis* he lavished some of his most fulsome rhetoric on the 'old world', which in its sunset had been fair to see, with its majestic 'princes and potentates', its secure ruling classes, and its splendid social pageantry. His later accounts, of the fall of the Romanovs, the dethronement of the Habsburgs, and the ruin of the Hohenzollerns, were no less grandiloquent. In *My Early Life* there was another lyrical lament for the vanished supremacies of the old nobility, in whose houses he had spent so much of his youth. The same theme was played out, with more eleborate variations, in the second chapter of the first volume of *Marlborough*. For over two hundred years, Churchill contended, it was a 'small and serious ruling class', consisting of 'several thousand families', which had produced the great captains and great statesmen who had been responsible for Britain's rise to world power. That was all now gone and 'our aristocracy', he lamented, 'has largely passed from life into history'.

This regret at the departed glories of the old regime received its fullest articulation on the death of 'Sunny' Marlborough in 1934. Churchill wrote a moving tribute in *The Times*, the theme of which was that the duke had lived out his sad life in admirable but vain defiance of the trends of twentieth-century history. On his accession to the dukedom, Churchill argued, 'the old world still existed', and 'in the glittering and it seemed stable framework of aristocratic society, he had a place where few were his equals and none his betters'. But in the years which followed, he went on, 'the organism of

English society underwent a complete revolution'; politics became 'more vehement and democratic'; 'successive crashes of taxation descended upon the old world'. The great governing families 'lost their authority and control'; were 'almost entirely relieved of their political responsibilities'; and were 'to a very large extent stripped of their property, and in many cases driven from their homes'. Inevitably, this regrettable process 'cast a depressing shadow upon the Duke of Marlborough's life'. He was 'always conscious that he belonged to a system which had been destroyed, to a society which had passed away', and understandably, this 'saddened and chilled him'.

This was, perhaps, an excessively apocalyptic view of the decline and fall of Churchill's own caste, the British aristocracy, though on the basis of his family experience it is easy to see why he felt and wrote as he did. Among his more distant relatives, the Churchills of Wychwood, the Cornwallis-Wests, the Frewens and the Leslies had all parted with their family houses and ancestral estates. Despite their Vanderbilt money, and the restoration of Blenheim, the Marlboroughs remained financially impoverished and socially unrespectable. Even Churchill's still super-rich kinsmen – the Wimbornes, the Westminsters and the Londonderrys – were no longer the territorial potentates or the political forces they once had been. For Churchill, this was a wholly regrettable development, and 'the disappearance of the aristocracy from the stage' was a trend which he rightly believed the Second World War further intensified. Like his ducal cousin, Churchill regarded the social structure that had existed in his youth as the best of all possible worlds.

He did not welcome aristocratic eclipse, but he could not prevent it. As Harold Laski perceptively noted in 1942, 'the premises of Mr Churchill's thinking are set by the old world that is dying'.

The other side of this lament for past glories was a growing disenchantment with parliamentary government as it had evolved during the twentieth century. By the inter-war years, Churchill was, like many disaffected and disoriented patricians, deeply alienated from the democratic process. He much regretted the granting of universal adult franchise in 1918, which he saw as the cause of all subsequent constitutional ills. The 'elegant, glittering, imposing trappings' had 'faded from British parliamentary life', and had been replaced by 'the caucus, the wire-puller and the soap box'. The great statesmen of his youth – Balfour, Rosebery, Morley, Asquith – had been followed by a new breed of insignificant pygmies: 'little men', vainly trying to cope with 'great events'. 'Real political democracy', as it had existed before 1914, had been superseded by a mass electorate, ignorant and volatile in its opinions, and easily swayed by an irresponsible press. Under these circumstances, it was not surprising that the Socialists had made such regrettable headway, that the prestige of parliament had markedly declined, that general elections produced violently fluctuating results, and that universal suffrage seemed totally discredited.

More to the point, Churchill believed that parliamentary government, thus decayed, could no longer deal with the seemingly intractable complexities of contemporary issues. As far as the handling of economic problems was concerned, Churchill set out his own proposals in his Romanes Lecture, delivered at Oxford University in June 1930. Since the Commons and the Lords were incapable of dealing effectively with such questions, the solution was to entrust them to a new economic sub-parliament, 'free altogether from party exigencies, and composed of persons possessing special qualifications in economic matters'. And as to the other tasks of government, the only hope was to improve the quality and standing of parliament by abandoning 'complete democracy'. In a series of newspaper articles, published during the early 1930s, Churchill developed this theme in more detail. The franchise should be moved away from one man one vote, back towards the traditional system which had been weighted in favour of the 'more responsible elements', by giving plural votes to householders and heads of families. Voting should be made compulsory, there should be proportional representation for great cities, and there should be a 'reformed and strengthened second chamber'. (This from the man who had once hailed the Parliament Act as 'territory reconquered by the masses from the classes'.)

During the 1920s and 1930s, Churchill was thus gradually developing into a reactionary class warrior, and came to share the widespread belief of disenchanted aristocrats that everything was going wrong, and that all change was change for the worse. From 1917 to 1922, he waged an impassioned but ineffectual campaign against the 'foul baboonery' of Bolshevism though, as Lloyd George wickedly but perceptively observed, one of the reasons for such obsessional hostility was that Churchill's 'ducal blood revolted against the wholesale liquidation of Grand Dukes'. At the time of the General Strike, Churchill further alienated working-class opinion by publicly assuming a belligerent posture against the trades unions, and by articulating it with such apparent enjoyment in the pages of the *British Gazette*. In his equally alarmist opposition to reform of the Indian government – where he was supported by such diehard grandees as Lord Salisbury and the Duke of Westminster – he once again placed himself in determined opposition to progress and democracy. By the mid 1930s, therefore, Churchill had become almost a parody of the paranoid aristocrat: intransigent, embittered, apocalyptic, 'a reactionary of the deepest dye', 'the chief exponent of the class war', and wholly without sympathy for the 'foreign and fallacious creeds of socialism'.

An even more ominous sign of Churchill's alienation from democracy was his growing interest in and admiration of authoritarian forms of government, especially the Fascist dictatorship. In 1926, he visited Italy, and immediately conceived a great admiration for the Duce's 'gentle and simple bearing'. In articles for British newspapers, Churchill praised Mussolini as a man of firmness, honour and destiny who, after a period of Bolshevik-inspired anarchy, was busy restoring Italy to her former greatness. For a time, indeed, a picture of the Duce was displayed at Chartwell, and on his return to the Commons Churchill was greeted with cries of 'Mussolini' by some MPs. In 1933 Churchill was still describing him in the press as 'the greatest lawgiver among men'. Four years later, he felt no doubt about 'the enduring position in world history which Mussolini will hold', as a result of the 'amazing qualities of courage, comprehension, self-control, and perseverance which he exemplifies'. Not surprisingly, given his trenchant criticisms of parliamentary democracy, Churchill was widely suspected, on both the left and the right, of wishing to become the British Duce: 'the potential Mussolini of a wave of reaction'.

There was certainly some domestic political evidence in support of this view. Ever since his time at the Admiralty, there were those who believed that 'at heart' Churchill was 'dictatorial' in his outlook. In the early 1930s, he hankered after an alliance with Oswald Mosley, whose youth and ebullience he much admired, and whose vision of a corporate state closely resembled that sketched out by Churchill in his Romanes Lecture. At about the same time, the pitifully déclassé Duke of Manchester published his autobiography, in which he expressed great admiration for Mussolini and urged in his concluding chapter that Britain needed a new leader, who would put an end to the pointless talking of parliament, and run the country with authoritarian benevolence as an aristocrat ran his landed estate. One of his candidates for that position was the seventeenth Earl of Derby. The other was Winston Churchill. In the same year, 1932, Harold Nicolson published a novel, *Public Faces*, which was set in the near future, and presumed that the country would by then be run by a Churchill-Mosley Coalition. Nor should it be forgotten that during the Second World War Churchill did indeed wield more absolute power than any Prime Minister before or since, and that even friends like Beaverbrook admitted that, in some moods, he had in him 'the stuff of which tyrants are made'.

In his political opinions, the authoritarian Churchill of the 1930s had clearly travelled a long way from the

Tory Democrat and the Liberal reformer of the 1900s. Since then, he had been a Lloyd George Coalitionist, a Baldwinite Conservative, and a Diehard reactionary. As Lord Beaverbrook once opined, he had held 'every view on every question'. But such erratic behaviour was far from being unusual between the 1880s and the 1930s, as many aristocrats found themselves adrift in the new hostile world of democratic politics, and boxed the political compass in essentially the same way. Some families split apart, like the Bedfords, the Trevelyans and the Mitfords, as one branch went to the right, others to the left. Some individuals moved with bewildering speed across the political spectrum: Whigs like Viscount Halifax became conservatives and then Diehards; the Buxton brothers moved from the Liberal Party to Labour; and Mosley went from Conservative to Labour to the British Union of Fascists. Here again, Churchill's apparently rootless behaviour was more typical of the declining aristocracy than is usually recognised.

Shortly after his illustrious cousin's death in 1965, Sir Shane Leslie predicted that the end of the twentieth century would have to be reached before Winston Churchill's astonishing career could be seen in its proper historical perspective. Having reached the early years of the twenty-first century, the wisdom of Leslie's prophecy seems to have been well borne out. That Churchill will occupy a conspicuous place in the history of his times seems certain – but until the pattern of that history has itself emerged more distinctly, the true nature of his own place within it is bound to remain unclear. Nevertheless, when any final reckoning is made, the fact that Churchill was an aristocrat, and the fact that for most of his life the aristocracy to which he belonged was in decline, will need to be given their due weight. Of course, there is a great deal that this will *not* explain about a personality so protean, so remarkable, so long-lived, so variously gifted, so internationally influential, and so much larger than life. But it will certainly help us to see him, and to understand him, as a historically credible figure to a greater degree than has hitherto been possible. Only by putting the Churchillian colossus in such a context can some of his true contours be discerned.

By viewing Churchill as the product of a declining aristocratic order, we can much better understand the doubts, the dislike and the distrust which he engendered for so much of his long political career. For it was not just that he was widely believed to be uncertain in judgement and unreliable in his political conduct. It was also that there was something about him more generally which was not entirely respectable. Labour politicians like Attlee and Bevin felt this; so did middle-class moralists like Reith, Baldwin and Neville Chamberlain. Although he was an aristocrat by birth, Churchill was widely believed to be not really a gentleman at all. On the contrary, he was often described as a highly gifted, but undeniable, 'cad'. Beyond any doubt, some of the more imaginative whispers – that he had broken his parole during the Boer War, that he was the creature of an international Jewish conspiracy, that he had fathered illegitimate children – were without factual foundation. But in the generally unseemly context of his family background and his own way of life, it is easy to see why such rumours adhered to him so tenaciously, and the political consequences of this in the years before 1939 should not be underestimated.

The aristocracy to which Churchill belonged, by connection and by inclination, was not that exemplified by such high-minded Christian gentlemen as Viscount Grey of Fallodon, Lord Halifax, or Sir Alec Douglas-Home, who stood for 'respectability' and 'spiritual values'. Nor was it the restful, intimate world of squirearchical estates, decaying manor houses, agricultural politics and village cricket. In terms of its characters and its orientation, Churchill's version (and vision) of aristocracy was romantic, raffish, restless, déclassé, metropolitan, plutocratic. Genealogically, financially and socially, he was on the edge. To be sure, he was not a 'typical' aristocrat: but in the course of his own lifetime, the aristocracy changed, adapted, dispersed and declined so much that it would be difficult to suggest anyone who was. Nevertheless, in terms of his ancestors, his family, his friends and his own way of life, he belonged to a recognisable (and highly suspect) stratum of aristocracy, which put Churchill at a distinct disadvantage for much of his political career.

All this makes it easier to appreciate why his advent to power in the spring of 1940 was greeted with such widespread doubt and dismay, as a man variously described as a 'cad', a 'half-breed', a 'dictator', a 'rogue elephant', the 'greatest adventurer in modern political history', took charge of Britain's affairs. It also enables us to understand the truly miraculous transformation in Churchill's reputation which the events of 1940–45 eventually brought about. The aristocratic anachronism became the embodiment of the bulldog breed. The drinker, the gambler, the spendthrift became a national 'character'. The impoverished patrician became, thanks to the sensational sales of his war memoirs and his *History of the English-Speaking Peoples*, financially secure. The incorrigible scrounger off family and friends became the deserving recipient of gifts, legacies, prizes and honours from a grateful world. The pot-boiling journalist and self-justifying family biographer became the Nobel Prizewinner for Literature. The belligerent class warrior, the man once likened to Mussolini, became the champion of freedom and liberty. The reactionary authoritarian became the saviour of his country. The ungentlemanly cad became the greatest Englishman of his time.

In an appropriately Churchillian manner, these antitheses are, no doubt, too crude. Before 1940, even his enemies grudgingly recognised that Churchill's larger-than-life faults were matched by at least some corresponding virtues; and after 1945, disagreeable rumours about his family, his friends and his finances continued to circulate (or be suppressed). But they also contain an essential and little-regarded truth. For the transformation in Churchill's image wrought by the Second World War should not obscure the very different, and much more damaging, reputation which he had acquired during the forty years which had gone before. And we cannot understand that earlier, more flawed, and more suspect Churchillian incarnation, unless we see him in the broader context of the declining aristocracy of which he was a product, and to which he never doubted for a moment that he belonged.

POCKET PENGUINS

POCKET PENGUINS

36. **Muriel Spark** The Snobs
37. **Steven Pinker** Hotheads
38. **Tony Harrison** Under the Clock
39. **John Updike** Three Trips
40. **Will Self** Design Faults in the Volvo 760 Turbo
41. **H. G. Wells** The Country of the Blind
42. **Noam Chomsky** Doctrines and Visions
43. **Jamie Oliver** Something for the Weekend
44. **Virginia Woolf** Street Haunting
45. **Zadie Smith** Martha and Hanwell
46. **John Mortimer** The Scales of Justice
47. **F. Scott Fitzgerald** The Diamond as Big as the Ritz
48. **Roger McGough** The State of Poetry
49. **Ian Kershaw** Death in the Bunker
50. **Gabriel García Márquez** Seventeen Poisoned Englishmen
51. **Steven Runciman** The Assault on Jerusalem
52. **Sue Townsend** The Queen in Hell Close
53. **Primo Levi** Iron Potassium Nickel
54. **Alistair Cooke** Letters from Four Seasons
55. **William Boyd** Protobiography
56. **Robert Graves** Caligula
57. **Melissa Bank** The Worst Thing a Suburban Girl Could Imagine
58. **Truman Capote** My Side of the Matter
59. **David Lodge** Scenes of Academic Life
60. **Anton Chekhov** The Kiss
61. **Claire Tomalin** Young Bysshe
62. **David Cannadine** The Aristocratic Adventurer
63. **P. G. Wodehouse** Jeeves and the Impending Doom
64. **Franz Kafka** The Great Wall of China
65. **Dave Eggers** Short Short Stories
66. **Evelyn Waugh** The Coronation of Haile Selassie
67. **Pat Barker** War Talk
68. **Jonathan Coe** 9th & 13th
69. **John Steinbeck** Murder
70. **Alain de Botton** On Seeing and Noticing